Unexplained Mysteries: Ancient Aliens Or Lost Technology?

The Missing Tech Behind The World's Greatest Structures

By: Robert Jean Redfern

© Copyright 2015 by Robert Jean Redfern - All rights reserved.

In no way is it legal to reproduce, duplicate, or transmit any part of this document in either electronic means or in printed format. Recording of this publication is strictly prohibited and any storage of this document is not allowed unless with written permission from the publisher. All rights reserved.

The information provided herein is stated to be truthful and consistent, in that any liability, in terms of inattention or otherwise, by any usage or abuse of any policies, processes, or directions contained within is the solitary and utter responsibility of the recipient reader. Under no circumstances will any legal responsibility or blame be held against the publisher for any reparation, damages, or monetary loss due to the information herein, either directly or indirectly.
Respective authors own all copyrights not held by the publisher.

Legal Notice:
This book is copyright protected. This is only for personal use. You cannot amend, distribute, sell, use, quote or paraphrase any part or the content within this book without the consent of the author or copyright owner. Legal action will be pursued if this is breached.

Disclaimer Notice:
Please note the information contained within this document is for educational and entertainment purposes only. Every attempt has been made to provide accurate, up to date and reliable complete information. No warranties of any kind are expressed or implied. Readers acknowledge that the author is not engaging in the rendering of legal, financial, medical or professional advice.

Table of Contents

Introduction	1
The Great Pyramid of Giza	4
Stonehenge	17
Goseck Henge	26
Derinkuyu Underground City	34
Pumapunku	41
Gobekli Tepe	47
Nan Madol	52
Hypogeum of Hal-Saflieni	66
Coral Castle	71
Russian Megalithic Stones	77
Conclusion	84

Introduction

Have you ever really dug into the facts on some of the ancient structures modern man has found over the years? If you have, you cannot help but be amazed at the engineering complexity, especially when you consider we cannot replicate some of these building mechanisms in the 21st century. So who really built structures like the great pyramid of Giza, Stonehenge, the underground city of Derinkuya, the mysterious Pumapunku, the Gobekli Tepe, and the underground Greek temple called Hypogeum of Hal-Saflieni?

Well, this fundamental question has been asked a thousand times and answered just as many. The problem, or perhaps confusion, with the answers is they are so tentative and diverse, which has only led to even more questions. Because, even though modern scientists, engineers, archeologists and the like have been relentlessly searching for the truth behind these amazing and mysterious presences we've found on our planet, who really knows what went on in the distant past? All each of us can do is look at the facts and form an opinion for ourselves that makes sense within the framework of what we consider feasible or possible.

Archeologists have been busy excavating fossils as evidence to back up their ever changing theories of when and who built these marvelous structures while scientists and engineers are preoccupied with trying to simply understand, never mind explain, the elaborate technology behind these ancient constructions. Could these structures be the woefully unappreciated achievement of ancient cultures? If so, how is it that this technology and the incredible building skills that went into erecting these structures simply vanished as time marched on? Or, were these wondrous engineering feats the handiwork of alien beings with vastly superior knowledge and the ability to move massive objects in ways far beyond the abilities of the civilizations they helped? If this is true, another question arises. Did these superior beings only visit the earth, or did they live among its inhabitants? Either way that question is answered, one must wonder: Why are they no longer visiting, or among us? Or are they?

In this book, we will look at several ancient structures and analyze the propagated theories about them as well as the underlying technology of the construction. With this information you will obtain a wider base of knowledge concerning ancient structures and even a more modern one, which will enable you to come to some sort of personal understanding of how these structures came about, and why they came to be on the planet Earth.

The Great Pyramid of Giza

Also known as the Pyramid of Khufu

Built Approximately: 2540 – 2560 B.C.

Location: Near Cairo Egypt

There are dozens of pyramid-shaped structures in Egypt with recent studies suggesting there are 118 to 138 in existence. The most famous of these pyramids are found in Giza, near Cairo. One of them, the Great Pyramid of Giza, also known as the Pyramid of Khufu, is one of the Seven Wonders of the World.

Structural features

-The geographic location of Khufu's pyramid is in the exact center of the earth's land mass, which means the Great Pyramid of Giza divides our globe into equal quarters. The image below that shows this phenomenon is from an original 1877 copy of Piazzi Smyth's "Our Inheritance in the Great Pyramid" by Charles Piazzi Smyth (1819-1900), who was a respected scientist and Astronomer Royal for Scotland.

- The Great Gaza pyramid of Khufu is perfectly aligned to True North, something even modern builders cannot accomplish. The closest we've come is within six degrees.

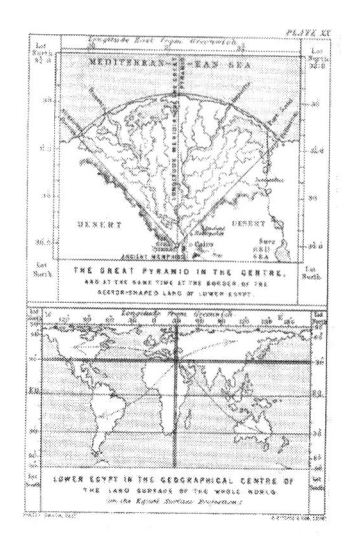

- This pyramid, at an original height of 481 feet, was considered the world's tallest man-made structure for more than 3,800 years.

-Each base side is 230.4 meters long (755.9 feet), and the relationship between Pi and Phi is expressed in the proportions of this pyramid.

-Considering the mass, volume and interior markings and references by the workers to a fourth dynasty pharaoh, Egyptologists conclude the structure was built over a 10 to 20 year period.

-The four faces of the pyramid structure are slightly concave to an extraordinary degree of precision making it appear, under certain lighting conditions, to have eight sides.

-The curvatures on the four faces exactly match the radius of the earth. Apparently this phenomenon is only visible from a height in the sky, and only at dawn and dusk at the time of the spring and autumn equinoxes when a shadow falls upon the structure.

-The pyramid consists of two and a half million blocks of stones weighing two to thirty tons each. The largest stones were granite and placed in the King's chamber. They weigh between 27 and 88 tons, and were transported from a quarry nearly 500 miles away.

-If the entire 20 years was used to build the Great Pyramid of Giza, more than 12 massive but perfectly sized blocks weighing tons each had to be placed with incredible precision into the structure every hour of every day and every hour of every night for a total of 175,200 straight hours. If the pyramid was built in only 10 years, 24 of these blocks had to be placed every hour! That means workers hoisted, maneuvered, lowered and precisely fit massive blocks weighing tons in no more than 2.5 minutes each. And they did it for 87,600 hours straight.

-The mortar used to build this pyramid has been analyzed and found to consist of known chemicals, but the composition cannot be reproduced. It is stronger than the stone and still holds today.

-The pyramid was originally covered with an outer mantle of 144,000 casing stones made of highly polished limestone that reflected the sun and moonlight like giant mirrors. So powerful was the light, it is said someone seeing it from the moon would have thought the glow was a star. Ancient Egyptians called this pyramid "Ikhet" which means "Glorious Light".

-The Great Pyramid of Giza has complex airshafts, passages and chambers. The entrance door, which weighed 20 tons and swiveled, was so well balanced and so precisely made that when the pyramid was first found, the door opened with only minimal force. Yet, when it closed, the fit was so perfect the door could hardly be detected. Wait until you get to see the underground network; the precise stonework is one of a kind.

-The coffer in the King's chamber was an enormous block of granite that would have required bronze saws 8-9 feet long with, they say, sapphire teeth. Under microscopic analysis, the coffer reveals it was fashioned using a hard, jewel bit drill at a drilling force of two tons.

Theories on how the Great Pyramid of Giza was built

There are mythical and both ancient and recent theories and hypotheses related to the pyramids existence-some remain as a hypothesis because no scientific evidence has been provided by the propagators.

Given the difficulty of construction, lack of engineering knowledge, difficulty of construction, and absence of sophisticated machinery, it seems fair to ask who built the Great Pyramid of Giza. Was it designed and constructed by the Egyptians, Satan, gods or aliens, and for what purpose? Some say Pyramids were hills that had mystic powers, or even foretell an apocalypse, while others saying Israelites wanted to steal the pyramids! Well, let's try to find out!

The Egyptians built the pyramids

Many scholars claim skilled crews of Egyptian men and women built the pyramids. Perhaps slaves were used, as well. Research indicates crews of 100,000 or more were used to construct something as large the Great Pyramid of Giza. Materials had to be transported over many miles, and perhaps using levers and other fairly primitive tools, they somehow managed to hoist huge stones and precisely place them to eventually create a complex structure that modern engineers and architects may not be able to replicate.

The proponents of this theory say Egyptians did not need cranes, lasers or aliens- they were simply well built strong men, so it's no surprise that they were able to carry heavy stones over long distances especially while working collectively. A carving of people pulling a huge statue found inside the pyramids is said to illustrate how they pulled heavy stuff and that they used pulleys to slide over 70 ton stones up to the top.

There is evidence that Egyptians cut stones-even granite or limestone – with a copper chisel and used desert sand as an abrasive for smoothing and polishing purposes. Recently, Barsoum said his experiments prove that the concrete mortar used by Egyptians is not an ordinary composition. Rather, it is made of silicon dioxide or a silicate mineral that we can't replicate today. Some say the stones were cast on the spot rather than dragged in from elsewhere up to the summit, and that explains why the stones fit together so perfectly.

Even if a massive and skilled work crew was available that was physically able to put forth the continuous herculean effort required to build this structure using primitive tools and brute strength, where did the engineering knowledge come from?

Ancient alien theory

Some researchers claim the ancient astronaut theory is at play in the evolution of human culture. They hypothesize that primitive man was enlightened by extraterrestrials that landed on our planet in space ships or flying saucers and jump-started a more sophisticated world civilization. Some UFO gurus such as Erich von Daniken of the 'Chariots Of The Gods' best seller book claim that just like the other ancient structures, pyramids were not triumphs of human engineering. Rather, aliens provided the wisdom, engineering know-how, and technology to build them. Some say aliens designed or built the Great Pyramid of Giza. Others say that although thousands of men could have had the ability to physically stack up large blocks of stones, one upon the other, the technology must have come from somewhere else in the form of ancient astronauts.

Aliens are said to have landed on earth using airstrips we see as weird marks called Nazca lines found on the ground in the Peruvian desert. Archeologists dismiss them as religious or irrigation symbols, but supporters believe that this extraterrestrial idea explains most of the baffling questions about ancient monuments. Some people claim to even have spoken to aliens telepathically and that they actually confirmed they built the pyramids and other ancient structures for concrete scientific purposes. How bizarre is that!

Why were the pyramids built?

Well, irrespective of who built them, the question that still remains is, why were they built? Here are some propagated assumptions as to why the pyramids were built:

1. The tomb of the king

It is commonly believed that the pyramids were built to be used as tombs for the pharaohs and their consorts during the kingdoms in the old and middle ages, though no bones of a dead pharaoh have been found yet.

2. Barrier against the desert sand

In 1845, a researcher claimed the pyramids were built to protect Egypt against sandy eruptions in the Egypt and Nubai deserts.

3. Imitations of the Noah's ark or the Tower of Babel

A researcher once claimed that the tower of Babel and the pyramids had similar dimensions that were borrowed from Noah's Ark. In 1859, a British researcher even claimed that Noah and not the Egyptians built the pyramids because he was most competent in the kind of mathematics used.

4. Filtering reservoirs

A philosopher in the 1800s once thought the pyramids were used to purify muddy water from the Nile, which passed through their passages.

5. To please women

This is quite a unique story. In the 19th century, a Mr. Gable claimed the structures were not built for geometrical purposes, but so that the ones who built them could intermarry with daughters of men.

6. Display of royal despotism

According to Aristotle, the king was persuaded by the priests to create work for the unemployed idling in the area. This would prevent them from turning mutinous or rebellious. Others thought that they were built to keep captives busy or to use up surplus money in the treasury.

7. To preserve knowledge from floods

Many Arab authors refer to this theory a lot. It is said that following a prediction of oncoming floods by astrologers, the pyramids were built to preserve the memory of existing learning. In addition, it was to preserve magic, medicines, and talismans.

8. To store grain

Yes, some believed they were Joseph's granaries-the Biblical one- which he made to store wheat during hard times.

Stonehenge

Built approximately: 3100 – 1600 B.C.

Location: Wiltshire England

Stonehenge is an arrangement of huge, rough, rectangular stones arranged in an interesting pattern set in a field near Wiltshire England. It has been a mystery ever since its discovery by modern man. There are no written records of whom and why these stones were schlepped on this particular spot. Since the middle ages, a number of wild theories have persisted about Stonehenge with some archeological, mythical, and paranormal explanations being brought forth.

Structural facts

-Each monolith (stone) is 2 meters high (6.6 feet) between 1 m and 1.5 m wide (3.3 – 4.9 feet) and approximately .8 m thick (2.6 feet).

-Stonehenge is aligned with the midwinter sunset and the midsummer sunset. It was also aligned with the most northerly setting and most southerly rising of the moon.

-Two types of stone were used to build Stonehenge: Sarsen stones that weighed 25 tons and were about 18 feet tall, and bluestones, a type of volcanic rock, brought in from 240 miles away that weighed up to four tons.

-It was suggested in 1771 by an astronomer named John Smith that the estimated total of 30 large sarsen stones of the outer circle multiplied by 12 astrological signs equaled 360 days of the year and the inner circle represented the lunar months.

-It took at least 30 million hours of labor to build, and some say it took approximately 1500 years.

-Stonehenge was built at least 300 years before the pyramids.

Theories on Who Built Stonehenge and Why

Those who built Stonehenge had to have been extremely sophisticated in mathematics and geometry.

Opinions differ on whether Stonehenge was built for ritual and burial activities or whether it was built as an astronomical observatory.

Some believe aliens built Stonehenge, but there is no proof of that, of course.

Some believe that the tall stones are actually grave markers.

Some people believe that Stonehenge is actually a giant clock.

Stonehenge is often referred to when people discuss crop circles.

Some of the more common theories about Stonehenge include: it was a religious place to worship; it was used for human sacrifice; it was a place of burial and cremation.

It's difficult to come to a definite conclusion about Stonehenge because more than half the stones are believed to be missing and many have fallen over.

Main Theories about Stonehenge:

Mythical theories

In the early ages, supernatural folktales heavily influenced historians' explanations. Records by Geoffrey of Monmouth around 1130 B.C. support a theory that claims the wizard Merlin, with the help of a giant, transported the magical stones from Ireland to build a burial place for Britain's dead princes. In 1655, John Webb, an architect, argued that Stonehenge was constructed to serve as a temple for Caelus (the Greek sky-god Uranus). Up until the late 19th century, the site was credited to the Saxons and other relatively recent societies. Still others claim the devil is responsible for the structure.

The Druids and other theories

In 1640, John Aubrey credited the druids for construction in his academic survey of Stonehenge. He made the first measured drawings of the site which really helped in later analysis. He demonstrated the calendrical and astronomical role in the stones' placement. In1740, an architect named John Wood undertook the first truly accurate analysis of Stonehenge and interpreted the site as being a place for pagan ritual, which was later challenged by Stukeley who saw druids as biblical patriarchs.

In the 19th century, John Lubbock attributed the site to the Bronze Age following the discovery of bronze object in barrows close to the monuments.

In more recent times, believers in UFOs have spun theories that ancient aliens built and used the site as a landing pad.

Radiocarbon dating

Radiocarbon dating of the site indicates construction of the monument started around 3100 BC and ended in 1600 BC. This eliminates some of the theories presented above. The popular druid's theory is watered down following evidence indicating that the Celtic society, which generated the druid priesthood, emerged much later, in 300 B.C. In addition, since the druids performed most of their rituals in the mountains or woods, they were unlikely to have used the site for sacrifices. Romans initially came to the British Isles in an expedition led by Julius Caesar in 55 B.C., much later than Stonehenge was constructed, and for this reason, theories suggesting Stonehenge was built as a Roman temple, are negated.

Scientific theories

A burial place

According to more recent studies, Stonehenge is believed to have initially been a cemetery for the elite. More than a century ago, archeologists exhumed bone fragments from the Stonehenge site, but at the time, they thought the remains were insignificant and reburied them. Now, more than 50,000 cremated bone fragments have been dug up by British researchers from where they were disposed. These bones represent 63 different individuals from Stonehenge. A documentary on BBC 4 revealed those buried at the site were an equal number of men and women along with some children.

According to Mike Parker Pearson, a researcher from the University College London Institute of Archeology, stones that mark the graves came from Wales. According to The Guardian newspaper, the archeologists also found a bowl and a mace head, which were probably used to burn incense. This suggests that those buried in the graves could have been the political or religious elite.

A place for healing

Another theory suggests that people from the Stone Age period considered the place had healing properties. In 2008, reports by archeologists Geoggrey Wainwright and Timothy Darvill indicated that many skeletons recovered around the Stonehenge site showed signs of injury or illness. The archeologist also reported finding some fragments of Stonehenge bluestones, the first stones erected on the site, which ancient people chipped to possibly use as talismans for healing or protective purposes.

A sounds cape

Steven Waller a researcher in archeoacoustics suggests that the circular Stonehenge construction may have been created to produce a sound illusion. Waller suggests that if two pipers were to play their instruments in a field, the strange effect would be noticed by a listener. The sound waves from the dual pipes would cancel each other out in some spots, creating quiet spots. A similar effect is created by Stonehenge, except that the stones block the sounds rather than creating competing sound waves.

A celestial observatory

Some claim those who built Stonehenge perhaps had the sun in mind and that during the summer solstice; the structure is aligned with the sun. Archeological evidence indicates pigs were slaughtered in December and January, which suggests that possibly rituals or celebrations were held around the summer solstice sunrise. The site also faces the winter solstice. Both solstices are celebrated even today.

A team building exercise

In 2012, Pearson, from the University College in London, claims that the construction period of Stonehenge coincides with the time Neolithic people increasingly began to unite. Pearson assumes they may have come together to celebrate during the solstices, and at some point decided to build the monument. He said since Stonehenge required pulling massive stones from as far as west Wales, then shaping and erecting them. Only the united effort of many people would have ensured success of the endeavor.

Goseck Henge

The German Stonehenge

Built: Approximately 5000 B.C.

Location: Gosneck, Germany

Gosneck is considered the oldest known solar observatory in the world – it is older than England's Stonehenge, even though the post holes at the English site are 1,000 years older. The picture above is the henge recreated in modern times on the exact spot it once existed.

Keep reading this section for information about how many ancient sites, even though they may have served different purposes, have been discovered to be connected.

Structural features
-The structure is 220 feet in diameter.
-The entrances are oriented towards the rising and setting winter solstice sun.
-Lies on the same latitude as Stonehenge and only a minute north of Stonehenge's longitude.
-Is one of 250 similar structures throughout Germany, Austria and Croatia, which is a relatively small area.
-It sits on one of two unique latitudes in the world at which the full moon passes directly overhead on its maximum zenith.

Theories about this Henge structure

Astronomy
Civilization at this time consisted of farmers using basic wooden tools. Even the markings on their pottery were

made with objects similar to forks, so it seems safe to assume they were not advanced peoples.

So how on earth were they capable of not only observing specific astrological events and capturing them in a structure made for viewing them, but then actually purposefully channel the light into a more powerful and focused beam by making progressively smaller entrances for the light to travel through? For what purpose?

Is it possible that these ancient cultures who only had primitive tools with which to carry out they agrarian lifestyle were astronomers?
At both this site in Germany and Stonehenge in English, people could watch the extremes of the sun and moon at right angles to each other even though the sites are 1400 miles apart. This particular phenomena is only possible within a band of less than one degree, of which Stonehenge (and Goseck) lies in the middle-third exact latitude at which the Midsummer Sunrise and Sunsets are at 90° of the Moons Northerly setting and Southerly rising.

Rituals

Bones indicating the flesh had been scraped off were found within the structure, leading to theories that this henge structure was also used for sacrificial rites or other purposes we can only imagine. Researchers originally thought the henge was a defensive structure because of the ditch around it. But since there are no structures within the perimeter within which to hide, they discarded the theory.

A Theory about Henges across the World

The interesting thing about the many henge sites around the world as well as other ancient sites that might include burial grounds, is that they seem to be part of a vast system of ley lines – or arteries through which the earth's magnetism circulates. These ley lines are known to most cultures by different names: 'Heilige Linien' to the Germans, 'Fairy paths' to the Irish, 'Dragon Lines' to the Chinese, 'Spirit Lines' to Peruvians and 'Song Paths' to the Australian Aborigines, as well as other names in different cultures around the world.

The Aborigines of Australia tell of a 'pastage', which they call the 'dream-time', when the 'creative gods' traversed the country and reshaped the land to conform with important paths called 'turingas'. They say that at certain times of the year these 'turingas' are revitalized by energies flowing through them which in turn, fertilize the adjacent countryside. They also say these lines can be used to receive messages over great distances. (http://www.ancient-wisdom.com/leylines.htm)

Ley lines are geometric, astronomical, magnetic (energy), or spirit alignments (as in funerary paths) that connect things like ancient monuments, structures, mounds and megaliths together across a distance of landscape.

One of the largest leys in England is called the St. Michael's Ley, which follows the path of the sun over a great distance, on a specific day of the year - the 8th of May – which is the spring festival of St. Michael. The ley line forms the hypotenuse of an enormous right angled triangle which aligns the three most sacred sites in England to a scarily precise work of geometry they say is accurate to within 1/1000th of whatever it is they measure with.

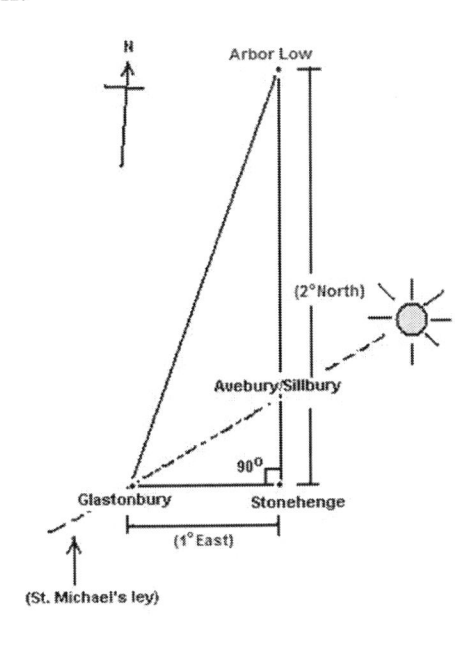

Image from: http://www.ancient-wisdom.com/stmichael.htm

These alignments can be found in many places across the globe between ancient structures. They indicate a deep knowledge of geometry, astronomy and Pythagorean theory that was taught in the earliest

Greek schools centuries after these sites were constructed.

The ley line in the image below is said to run from Ireland all the way to Jerusalem.

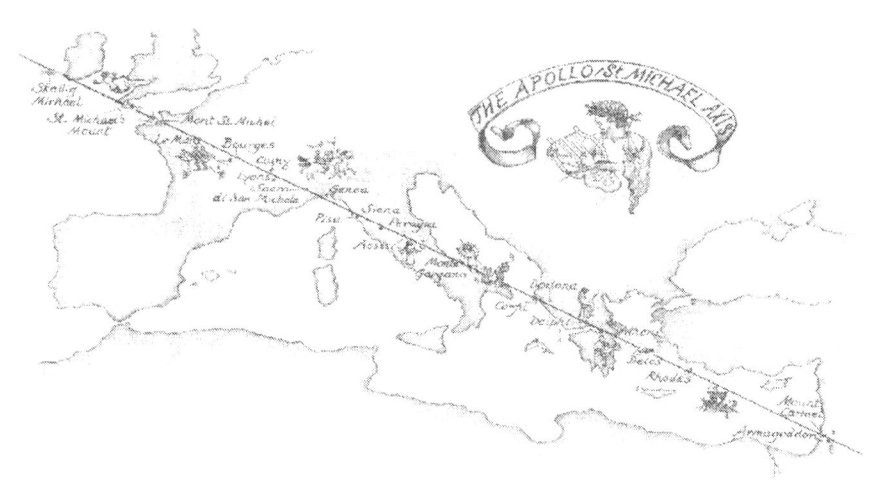

From: http://www.ancient-wisdom.com/leylines.htm

So what does this all mean?

If one entered a deep study of ancient structures on a global scale, noting placement and proximity to other sites while taking in astronomical events across a landscape, it would be hard to deny that there must have been some serious aerial viewing going on. Or at the very least, a very comprehensive understanding of the geography over vast distances. It would also have to include things like survey work and other ways to line up things vast distances away since there would be no visual on-the-ground line of sight help to be had.

How on earth could primitive man have achieved THAT feat? For that matter, why would it even occur to civilizations that were still having trouble making pottery and useful tools, to connect their structures in a way that recognized the sun moving across an entire continent on a specific day?

Are we back to thinking there might have been some help from ancient astronauts?

Derinkuyu Underground City

Built approximately: 1400 – 800 B.C. or (as one theory suggests), before the last Ice Age which began 110,000 years ago

Location: Cappadocia region of Turkey

Derinkuyu is an ancient and massive multi-level underground city discovered in 1963 in the Cappadocia region in Turkey. This region contains many other underground cities like Kaymakli.

Brief history

During a simple renovation of a modern house above the ground, a cave wall opened revealing an awe-inspiring vast city more than 283 feet deep, big enough to accommodate over 20,000 people along with their livestock. To the relief of everyone present, the underground city was abandoned and there were no strange creatures swarming inside.

Derinkuyu is the largest excavated city in Turkey and it was hidden right under everyone's' nose for many centuries. It's hard to tell how old the city is since stones cannot be carbon dated. However, it's thought to have been constructed around in the 8th—7th century B.C.

Structural features

-With an area of over 10.4 kilometers (6.4 miles) square, Derinkuyu has miles of tunnels connecting it to other underground cities in the region.

-It has 13 floors approximately 85m (approximately 279 feet) in depth.

-There are15,000 airshafts, escape routes, separate doors and many activity chambers which include living quarters, communal rooms, wineries, arsenals, tombs and stables for livestock and store rooms.

-The city has underground fresh water well systems, a security system made of enormous rolling stone doors that open from the inside and each level could be sealed using the same system from the next level.

-This structure is carved into an underground rock and even after so many years, it is still strong enough to host guests such as tourists and archeologists.

-Although the building stone is relatively soft, the entire site has never experienced any cave-ins suggesting that whoever built this structure possessed advanced knowledge of stone, stone network, engineering, architecture and local geography.

One not only wonders how, but also why, this complex underground facility was built. No construction records exist and the inhabitants during that time either moved to other areas or vanished. This structure remains a mystery to this day although many religious, mythical, and scholarly theories have emerged trying to explain this city.

Theories for Derinkuyu

Here are the major assumptions:

Ancient Christian's theory

Underground cities are said to have been occupied by many cultures over the centuries and early Christians are among the most recent group to stay at the caverns, but assuming they built the cities would be a stretch.

Monarchical activities in Cappadocia are believed to have started around the 4th century B.C. and according to UNESCO, it's around this time Kayseri (the great bishop of Caesarea) is said to have instructed the small anchoritic communities to inhabit cells dug into the rock. In order to resist Arab forays, the communities later began to unite into villages or subterranean towns such as Derinkuyu and Kaymakli, which served as refuge places

Some researchers suggest Phrygian people could most probably be behind the construction of this city since they occupied the area around 800 B.C.

Another theory suggests that the city was built around the 14th century B.C. by Hittites who were retreating from a Phrygian invasion, according to the "encyclopedia of architectural engineering feats".

King Yima theory

Some researchers suggest that the underground city could be much older than the Christian era and claim Persian King Yima constructed the caves. He is believed to have been more a mythological figure than an actual king who had a lifespan of more than 900 years similar to the Christian Bible's kings. If familiar, this story is similar to the Noah's story in the Christian Bible.

According to the Zoroastrian text "Vendidad", thestory goes that Ahura Mazda,a god, ordered Yima to construct an underground city to protect his people from a catastrophic winter. The king was instructed to assemble the best people and animals in pairs as well as the best seeds in order to reseed the earth once the winter disaster passed.

The "Vendidad" was composed many centuries ago and possibly originated before the 8th century B.C., but many of these stories could have been passed on through oral traditions way before that.

If this assumption is true, and indeed, the "Vendidad" is referring to this city, the last ice age occurred around 110,000 to 10,000 years ago, which means that the construction of Derinkuyu happened during remote pre-history.

Built For Protection

Other researchers suggest the structure was built as protection from invading forces. This theory is strongly supported by the labyrinth security doors, escape routes and underground wells to prevent poisoning. However, it would have taken a long time to build the vast network without advanced tools. In addition, if they were working under the threat of invasion, the masons would have hada very limited time frame to complete such an enormous task and the craftsmanship behind this structure also suggests otherwise. It's also possible that although the network was built hastily at first, each group that followed could have added to the levels over and over again.

Ancient Aliens Theory

Recently, UFO researchers claim that the complex technology behind this construction could not be the work of a primitive Stone Age man's tools and that advanced technology was used or brought here by alien astronauts who visited earth during prehistoric times. Well, no one knows for sure.

Pumapunku

Built approximately: 536–600 A.D.

Location: near Tiwanaku, Bolivia.

Pumapunku is an ancient and mysterious city in Bolivia, South America whose remains were recently discovered. This area is important in Inca traditions because they believe it is where the world was created. This site is an enigma, because no one really knows who built the structure, although it's commonly said to have been built by Tiwanaku people. It's not any ordinary old city; the thing that sets it apart is the extreme precision of the stone work applied, which would give modern builders a run for their money.

Structural features

- The way the city was constructed, shaped and positioned is unique and intriguing. The walls of Pumapunku were made from giant rock slabs shaped into jigsaw-like puzzle pieces with perfect right angles that were fitted together to create strong, load bearing joints that didn't require mortar.

-The cuts are so precise, even a razor blade cannot be inserted between some of the rocks. The stones were shaped so precisely and are so similar; it suggests mass production or prefabrication.

-Some of the site's unfinished rocks show that stone hammers were used to pound the stones which were then polished with sand and flat stones until they were as smooth as glass. There are very few such perfectly flat surfaces on earth. You would think lasers or machine tools were used in cutting them, but there is no evidence that this ancient civilization had the use of such modern apparatus.

-The I-cramps metals used to protect the building from shattering in the event of an earthquake is similar to what masons use today.

-The megalithic stones found on the site are some the largest on earth weighing over 100 tons each and measuring up to 29 feet long and 17 feet wide, equal to over 20 standard semi- trailers

-Archaeologists believe each stone was transported up a steep incline from a quarry near Lake Titicaca, roughly 10 kilometers (6.2 miles) away.

-Pumapunku's stonework and facing consists of red sandstone and a mixture of andesite. Clay is at the core of the structure, but river sand and cobbles are at the edges.

-The granite and diorite stones used in this site mean only diamond-tipped tools could have cut through the stones, or at least very advanced machinery.

-To sustain the weight of these huge structures, the foundation of Pumapunku was meticulously built by either digging trenches and layering sedimentary rocks inside or fitting stones directly to the bedrock. Modern engineers call this technique layering and depositing.

-The city is located at an altitude of 12,800 feet, above the natural tree line.

Here are some assumptions on who built Pumapunku:

Tiwanaku people

Assuming the theory that the Tiwanaku people built this structure, there are still some fundamental questions left half answered. At such a high altitude, it clearly indicates that trees could grow. Consequently, there wasn't anything available with which to create wooden rollers to transport these huge stones. According to archeologists, these huge stones were carried from quarries 6 - 60 miles away from the site.

Now, the key question is "how did they transport the stones? If the Tiwanaku people were behind this construction, without cranes, wheels or even a writing system, how were they able to move these giant rocks and shape them into such perfectly complex forms? Archeologists claim that their large labor force somehow did it using lama skin ropes, ramps and inclined planes. Just like any other ancient civilization, the Tiwanaku mysteriously vanished, the empire that followed (The Inca), even considered them to be gods because of their extremely impressive work.

Ancient alien theory

The more than 1000 year old ruins indicate precise workmanship was applied using very advanced equipment which was not available to this ancient culture at the time. The supporters of the alien theories claim that either ancient extraterrestrial built the site, or deities who were actually aliens helped the ancient people build it.

Built for religious purposes

Some theories as to why it was built claim Pumapunku and the surrounding temples were used by the Tiwanakus as ritual and spiritual centers. The site is said to have been visited by pilgrims from far away areas to marvel at its beauty. The peak of the nearby mountain called Illimani was considered sacred, and home to spirits of the dead. Therefore, the ancient Tiwanakus could have purposely integrated Pumapunku into this mountain site.

Gobekli Tepe

Built approximately: 10,000 B.C.

Location: Southeastern Anatolia Region of Turkey near Şanlıurfa

Gobekli Tepe is in Turkey, and considered the world's first temple. It was constructed about 12,000 years ago. Carbon dating traces the site to 10,000 B.C., which is older than the pyramids and Stonehenge by 6000+ years, and even pre-dates pottery. It was discovered in 1963, but considered just a medieval cemetery until

Professor Klaus Schmidt and other German archeologists began excavations in 1995.

Structural features

-The site is seen as oval shaped with circular structures on a hill top, but wait until you see the details.

-Excavations show the structure has at least 20 temples, each having two big monumental pillars at the center and more pillars in the walls.

-The identical, T-shaped limestone pillars measure up to 6 meters (20 feet)high, and weigh 40- 60 tons. They are perfectly fitted into the bedrock and arranged in circular rings.

-The pillars' flat surfaces have carvings of animals like foxes, cranes or snakes, and some have abstract symbols and predator sculptures.

-The structure was found buried deep for preservation purposes.

Theories on how and why it was built

Ancient cultures ritual or sacred grounds

It's commonly believed that ancient cultures built Gobekli, but there are no clear details on how they did it. It is still a mystery how this ancient culture, who had limited access to even hand tools, built this complex structure. How did they move, and then erect, the huge stone pillars? The evidence indicates these people didn't practice agriculture or live in a settlement. Recent discoveries show this place was not always as dry as it is now; back in the day, it was a flourishing paradise that had game, nut trees, wild grains, and fruits so they did not need to practice farming. There is no evidence of domestics such as garbage dumps, houses or hearths, so clearly people didn't settle here. In those times, nobody could write, read or construct anything apart from working with hides.

Archeologists are still puzzled as to how these hunters and gatherers built such an enigma without organization and resources. Conventional knowledge claims farming predates building, but agriculture is said to have started in this region a few centuries after Gobekli was built. The kind of architectural magnificence displayed on the site is equated to that of other megalithic structures. This makes one wonder when civilized human history really began.

Archeologists suggest that the symbolism on the site, the temples, and numerous animal-like bones provide sufficient evidence that the site was used for religious or ritual purposes. One said that the depictions of vultures show that the site was perhaps a death cult residence. They claim that it must have been religion rather agriculture that inspired the original dwellers to built this structure.

The site is still under excavation, so hopefully more compelling evidence will emerge with time.

It's the Garden of Eden

Author Tom Knox, in a recent article in the daily mail, came up with the hypothesis that this vast and complex monument might have been the allegorical Garden of Eden. He points out that this place was once between the Tigris and Euphrates rivers, and in fact, history began here, and this is where people were forcefully evicted to till the land and fend for themselves. The Christian Bible has the full story. Scientifically, this theory proposes that this ancient site was perhaps the 'turning point' of our social evolution-where modern agriculture was born, which makes it a bit convincing.

A lost civilization built it

Graham Hancock, also a broadcaster, claims a 'third party' or lost civilization once existed and was possibly wiped out by global cataclysm 10,000 years ago. Perhaps they were behind the construction of Gobekli and other impressive structures. Hancock says the structures built by this civilization were actually older than what archeologists assert.

Alien theory

As usual, if you can't explain it, blame it on the aliens! The same extraterrestrial explanation has applied to these structures.

Nan Madol

Built:Around 800 - 900 A.D. or 12,000 years ago (same suspected age of the underwater ruins found off the coast of Yonaguni, Japan) depending on who you listen to. Carbon dating seems to have been ineffective at this site.

Location: Pohnpei Island in Micronesia in the Western Pacific Ocean

Nan Madol is the only ancient city ever built in the ocean. The structures were constructed on top of artificial islands made of coral reefs. It is situated on the far eastern end of an island called Pohnpei, which is a little bigger than New York City. Pohnpei Island is part of what is now called the Federated States of Micronesia. This group of more than 1,000 little islands is fairly close to the Philippines to the West, and nearly 2,500 Southwest of Hawaii. Nan Madol sits very close to the equator.

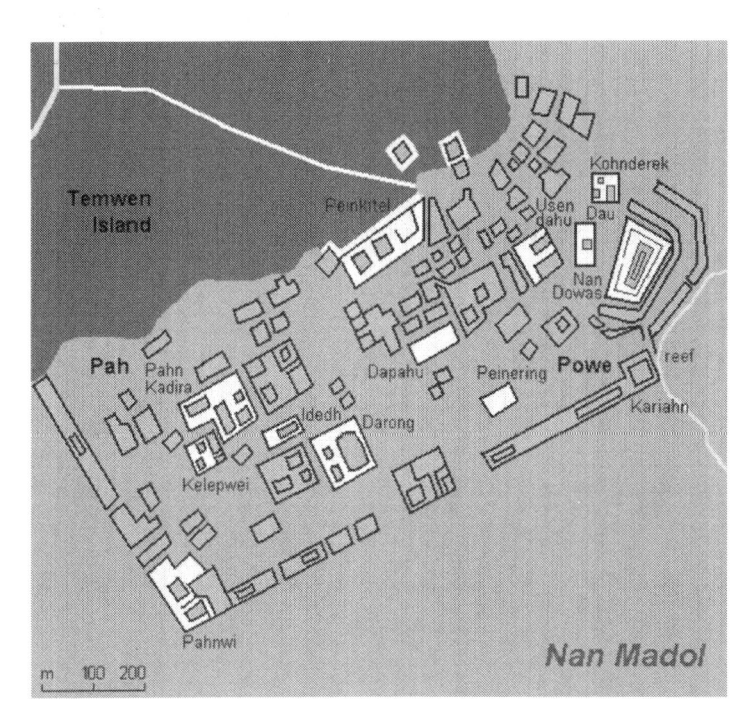

Image is from the Christopher Pala's article

Structural features

- Consists of 92 artificial islands (islets) over 11 square miles

- Made of coral filled platforms and magnetized basalt crystal stone structures surrounded by tidal canals.

- The more than 250 million stones used to construct the city are basalt logs broken from volcanic rock weighing from five to 50 tons each.

- Exact origin of stones has never been determined, but they are not local. The stones had to be transported in.

- Stone walls enclose an area approximately .93 miles long (1.5 km) by 3 blocks wide (0.5 km).

- The basalt logs were stacked log cabin style in a marvel of ancient engineering so complex nobody can figure out how they did it.

- Scuba divers continue looking for an escape tunnel bored down through the reef reported to be at the center of Nan Madol.

- All food and water had to be brought into Nan Madol by boat.

- Dubbed the Eighth Wonder of the World.

There are quite a few interesting things about Nan Madol

First of all, why build a city entirely on top of the ocean rather than on land where they are usually located? Especially if you have to build islands upon which to put the city?

The name Nan Madol means "spaces between" which, of course, is a reference to how the city was erected inside a lagoon on separate islands that had water in-between them, much like the water canals of Venice. Its original name was Reef of Heaven.

The biggest mystery after how these ancient peoples were able to built artificial islands in the ocean is how the heavy stones and columns got there in the first place.

Rufino Mauricio is Pohnpei's only archaeologist and he has dedicated his life to studying and preserving the ruins. In his expert opinion he says that given the size of Pohnpei's population at the time – fewer than 30,000 people – the construction of Nan Madol is an even larger and more remarkable effort than the Great Pyramids were for the ancient Egyptians.

It has been determined that none of the local quarry sites produced the megalithic magnetic basalt crystal logs that form the city's structures. These logs were created from volcanic rock that naturally breaks to form long, log-like blocks. This means all these rock-logs had to be transported onto the island from somewhere else.

That might not seem too impossible until you realize these stones each weighed between five and 50 tons, and with walls up to 17 feet wide and 50 feet tall, it means they would have had to move more than 250 million pieces of these rock-logs to build Nan Madol. Can you image toting and floating them across the ocean on a raft?

I think not. In fact, when the Discovery Channel was making a documentary about Nan Madol in 1995 they tried to replicate transporting stones over the water and found that anything weighing more than one ton would be impossible to move in this way. So how did the stones get there?

Theories on How Nan Madol Came To Be

Black Magic

Well, many of the modern day locals who live on the island believe the stones were flown to the island using black magic. According to Pohnpeian legend, twin brothers Olisihpa and Olosohpa from a mythical place called Kanamwayso arrived one day in a large canoe. They were looking for some place special to build a temple from which they could worship Nahnisohn Sahpw, the god of agriculture.

Did I mention these brothers were sorcerers? It is said these brothers levitated the huge stones used to build Nan Madol with the aid of a flying dragon.

In time, as legend has it, Olisihpa died of old age and his brother married a local woman and became the first of the Saudeleur dynasty which reigned over Nan Madol for 12 generations.

There are no written records of this place. In fact, locals claim the ruins are under a spell and won't go near it. Beyond that, though, they believe anyone who *does* talk about it will surely die, just like Governor Victor Berg did in the early 20th century. He defied the local king's decree about disturbing the holy ground. He entered the sealed tomb of one of the ancient island rulers on Nan Madol and found skeletons of giants 7 to 10 feet tall at which point a tumultuous storm arose with vicious lightening splitting the skies and torrential rains slashing the black walls of the city.

Governor Berg fell sick with a fever and spent a delirious night. The next morning, April 30, 1907, he was dead. The island physician, of course, could not determine the cause of death.

Theories on the giants

Who were these giants Governor Berg found? Some say they came from the lost continent of Lemuria dating back 12,000 years. Some say those giants who lived on

Nan Madol consisted of three distinct species of giants: one was human-like with an ability to fly; one could both fly and live under the sea; and the last was a breed of "mega giant" that was described as a class of worker-drones who labored under the ocean.

To support this, in the early nineteen hundreds researchers in the area recorded a legend about the Kona, a cannibalistic race of giants. Today that legend has become scaled down to the sorcerer brothers Ohlosihpa and Ohlosohpa who, it is said, fed on their island subjects.

In 1928 the Japanese took the platinum caskets from the House of the Dead under the sea at Nan Madol so there is no hope of checking DNA at this point to discover more about these giants.

Built by Aliens

Some say Nan Madol was built by aliens.

Could ancient astronauts have used technology beyond our comprehension to transport those massive stone logs? Did they impart advanced engineering knowledge to humans that was way beyond the construction capabilities of the time?

I guess we'll never know.

Built by an ancient culture from Lemuria

Another interesting theory can be found in Frank Joseph's book called "The Lost Civilization of Lemuria." He explains that Nan Madol was built by a past civilization from Lemuria – a continent that sunk after being onslaught by the forces of Mother Nature. The Lemurians used technology to work *with* the natural processes of the earth and not against it as modern man seems to do.

Before we get into his theory, here is a summary of Nan Madol.

-It is built on a coral reef about five feet above sea level between the equator and the eleventh parallel and made out of more than 275 million tons of prismatic magnetized basalt spread over 170 acres.

-The basalt is magnetized in an unusual manner, which Joseph says is important and intentional. Conventional, mainstream scholars have not yet figured out how Nan Madol was made, who built it, where the building materials came from, and for what purpose it was built.

-Sea level analysis and studies of the sediment on the ocean floor in this area as well as examinations of surrounding semi-submerged ruins at the base of Nan Madol and surrounding waters put the approximate date for construction at approximately 12,000 years ago. This is based on the concept that the last time the ruins that are currently underwater would have been on dry land and above sea level is approximately 12,000 years ago.

-Nan Madol is positioned between Hawaii and the Philippines at a location where severe storms and typhoons are generated by cold air brought into contact with the warm waters of the Caroline Islands near Nan Madol. Think of this: because severe storms originate in this spot, Nan Madol would rarely be *hit* by storms; therefore it is the safest place in the Pacific Ocean. Now take it a step farther and realize that the major contributing effect to typhoons and hurricanes is electromagnetic energy, even more so than the temperature of the water. Prove this to yourself by considering that the warmest ocean temperatures should be at the height of summer in any given region – July and August in America – but peak hurricane season is September through October, and even into November when waters are cooler.

-Platinum and silver 'bars' were found within Nan Madol.

-The area around Nan Madol has unique and constant subtle seismic activity. Joseph says seismic activity generates piezoelectricity which works with the strangely magnetized basalt to focus a concentrated coronal discharge skyward.

Now, considering the location of Nan Madol, the unique and intentionally altered magnetism of the basalt and the layout of the ruin, it can easily be argued that Nan Madol was an ancient site using weather manipulation technology to diffuse dangerous storms before they built up.

The coronal discharge let off by the magnetized basalt generated by piezoelectricity from the island's constant subtle seismic activity means Nan Madol could react with a storm's electromagnetic elements.

Nan Madol, by nature of its construction could effectively diffuse storms.

But wait!

Alien Theory

How could less than 30,000 natives with no knowledge of advanced engineering techniques not only build artificial islands and then erect this massively heavy fortress of stone over open ocean, but potentially manipulate electromagnetic frequencies and acoustic resonance (used at Stonehenge, too) to save themselves from approaching storms.

Nan Madol appears to be an example of ancient lost technology. Was it brought here by aliens, or built by an ancient Lemurian civilization with considerably more technological expertise than we have today?

We'll never know, but it's something to think about.

Hypogeum of Hal-Saflieni

Built approximately: 3300 – 3000 B.C.

Location: Paola, Malta

Hypogeum of Hal-Safleini is found in Paola, Malta and is in the famous UNESCO's world heritage list. It was accidently discovered around 1902 by workers cutting cisterns for a new house that broke through its roof. It dates back to around 3300-3000 B.C., before the first stone of the pyramids was cast. Often, it's simply referred to as Hypogeum meaning underground in Greek, and the only known temple found in prehistoric times. Around 7000 human remains were found during excavations in the 1990s.If you'd like to tour this unique site, book in advance since only 60 people are allowed to enter per day.

Structural features

Hypogeum has over 30 rooms and three levels made of limestone, plus halls and many passages.

First level

This level is 10 meters (nearly 33 feet) underground and similar to the nearby tombs. Some of the rooms found here are natural caves while others were extended artificially.

Second level

The mid chambers were apparently created to align with the setting of the sun. This level was opened because the first was no longer adequate and has rooms of some importance:

-Main chamber - appears almost circular and carved from a rock with many trilithon doors leading to other chambers and red ochre walls. Statuettes of the sleeping lady were found here.

-A fancy room - decorated with geometrical spiral patterns; circular, very spacious with inward slanting, even walls, and a carving of a human hand, seen on the right wall as you enter.

-An oracle room-the smallest chamber and roughly rectangular-the powerful acoustic sounds produced from any vocalization inside it makes it most peculiar; also painted with the beautiful spirals and circular artwork.

-A 2 meter (6.5 feet) deep snake pit - a structure supposedly used for snake collection.

- Holy of holies - a space with two large vertical stones with two thick layers of trilithon and a corbelled ceiling. This chamber is aligned with the winter solstice.

Third level

This level had no evidence of offerings or bones, only water, which suggests it was a granary.

Theories on Who built the Hypogeum and Why

Maltese Community

The Maltese community is said to have built the structure using stone mallets, horn or antler picks, and the walls were most likely smoothed using imported flint. Of course, some people don't believe this was possible. Archeologists say the human and animal bones indicate sacrifices and burial rituals took place here.

Some say it was a place of magic, initiation rites or incubation, evident in the sleeping woman's body at Valletta museum. It is claimed that if a dead person were buried in the chamber, he/she would be resurrected. Burial rituals are said to have taken place here.

But others say it was a temple which later became a tomb. The perfect acoustics were used by the living, not the dead, say musicians. Some say the hand on the wall signifies this place is a doorway to talk to dead ancestors or to reach deities, and that initiates were asked to spend a night in the dark temple to get insight from deities who keep in touch with humans.

No one really knows whether it was a temple or a tomb. In case you visit this place, be careful you don't get lost. It is vast and spooky.

Coral Castle

Built: in the early 1900's

Location: Homestead, Florida, United States of America

Coral Castle, while not an ancient structure, is considered an engineering marvel and compared with Stonehenge and the Great Pyramids of Egypt. Even more amazing is the fact that it was built by just one man: a Latvian immigrant, Edward Leedskalnin, who was just 5 feet tall and weighed 100 pounds.

It is not really a large castle like you see nestled in the mountains of Germany, and it's not really made of coral. But it is world famous because, using only simple tools, Leedskalnin quarried, sculpted and stacked more than 1,000 tons of sedimentary oolite limestone (into which coral had imbedded itself) into interesting shapes like chairs, a crescent moon, sundial, water fountain, stairs and a rather tall building.

The largest stone weighs 28 tons.

Many sources claim that the castle, originally called Rock Gate Park, is scientifically inexplicable. According to the attraction's website, "Coral Castle has baffled scientists, engineers and scholars since its opening in 1923.

Legend has it that Leedskalnin was inspired to build the castle after being jilted by his 16 year old bride-to-be. He wanted to prove he could do something incredible, despite being poor and uneducated.

Theories on How It Was Built

How was he able to hoist and precisely stack the large blocks seen in the photos?

And how could he build the 9-ton door that swiveled quietly open at the touch of a finger? It wasn't until the late 1980's when it quit working and was taken apart that contractors realized a bar ran through the stone that sat upon a truck bearing which allowed it to swivel.

Even after careful repairs using current technologies and tools, though, nobody has ever been able to make it work as smoothly as it did originally. Today, it takes more than a mere finger to move the massive rock.

Psychic Powers, Sound Waves, Occult Practices or Earth Energies

Many stories and wild theories have emerged over the decades about Leedskalnin and how he built his castle. Some say that, in front of witnesses, he levitated the blocks with psychic powers. Others say he did so by singing to the stones. Still others suggest Leedskalnin had arcane knowledge of magnetism and so-called "earth" energies.

We do know Leedskalnin was involved with the Masons, and the castle is replete with Masonic symbolism which seems to fuel imaginations who say the man who created this place had inside knowledge of forgotten occult practices.

Leedskalnin himself would only say, ""I think I have figured out how they built the pyramids." Unfortunately, that knowledge died with him in 1951.

Alien Technology

Others say he was privy to alien technologies and that's why he only worked at night when he thought nobody could see what he was doing.

Today, this "castle" could be constructed rather easily with a construction crew in possession of cranes and other modern machinery. But this builder worked alone with only simple pulleys and winches that are displayed on the site along with an odd looking device that some speculate could have been an all-magnet motor, possibly involved in levitation work.

There are always two sides to any story, especially when, from our 21st century perspective we think of our technology and the massive machinery now available. It seems it would be a cinch to build such a "castle."

But this was a small man working alone with primitive tools. How did he move a 28 ton rock around?

To many, applying the principles of leverage are not enough to explain Coral Castle. Was its creator in touch with the forces of the universe? Perhaps he was privy in some way to alien technologies. Or maybe he was visited by ancient astronauts who shared some of their secrets.

Russian Megalithic Stones

(Look for the man on the ledge to get an idea of how massive this wall is)

Built: Awaiting Testing to Determine
Location: Mount Shoria, Southern Siberia - Russia

In the last few years, an incredible collection of Megalithic granite stones forming a huge wall was discovered on Mount Shoria in southern Siberia. In fact, the site was explored for the first time in 2013.

This massive wall of megothilic granite stones could shatter conventional theories about the history of our planet. And, could this Russian site be evidence of an ancient civilization our history is unaware of?

Some of these stones are estimated to weigh more than 3,000 tons and appear to be cut with flat surfaces, right angles and sharp corners.

Some crazy stuff was happening while on the site. So much so that people in the expedition called it "mystical." The geologist's compasses were behaving very strangely. For unknown reasons, the arrows on the compasses pointed away from the megaliths. So the geologists speculate this means the megoliths were exhibiting "an inexplicable phenomenon of the negative geomagnetic field."

Some wonder: could this be a remnant of ancient antigravity technologies?

How could people cut these giant stones with precision, transport them up the side of a mountain and then stack them more than 131 feet high?

In the commonly accepted version of history it would have been *impossible* for ancient humans with their limited ideas of technology and the primitive tools they worked with to accomplish this feat.

Is there more going on behind the scenes in the distant past of our planet than meets the eye?

The super megaliths were found and photographed for the first time by Georgy Sidorov on a recent expedition to the Southern Siberian Mountains.

Although the site needs much more research as to their age and construction, someone involved with the find said he believes the megaliths stretch way back into the "pre-history mists of time."

Theories as To How the Wall Was Built

Mother Nature Did It

Apparently some scientists claim this rock formation is the result of "geological processes that include intense weathering of the rock."

They say both tectonic forces acting on deeply buried bedrock and pressure releases that occur near surface bedrock as it is uplifted and eroded, can form rectangular, block-like, rock formations that consist of jointed rock.

As the bedrock is uncovered by erosion, they say, these joints – known as orthogonal joints – can intersect at exactly 90 degrees, creating formations comparable in size and shape to alleged megaliths such as this wall.

Scientists do try to stay away from anything remotely close to "mystical," but it seems strange when looking at the photographs to think Mother Nature would go about stacking huge, geometrically precise pieces of herself after making sure the edges were relatively smooth.

Some of us might tend to disagree with the scientists who, after all, do try to appear practical.

Ancient Civilization

Obviously there is speculation as to whether a civilization existed long before recorded history that had the ability to literally move mountains. Time and research will tell.

Aliens Again

Given the magnetic properties displayed at the site with the geologists compasses, one can't help but wonder if something happened here that can never be explained within the scope of our understanding.

Conclusion

The structures discussed here are in no way a comprehensive list of what is scattered around the world. They only serve to give you a glimpse into the ancient building technology that seems to have disappeared with the builders.

Other sites include The Greater Gyzgala, Sigiriya in Sri Lanka, The Trilithon at Baalbek, Nazca lines in Peru, Sacsayhuamán, The Great Dam of Marib, Sacsayhuaman in Peru, the Chavin de Huantar Ruins in Peru, The Lost City of Mohenjo-Daro in Pakistan, Chogha Zanbil in Iran and The Great City of Teotihuacán.

All these ancient structures leave modern man in awe, for the science of archeology tells us that even if the people of these ancient cultures somehow had amazing insights into advanced engineering principles, they didn't have the tools or machines to bring such advanced structures into being.

Ancient cultures didn't have huge backhoes with which to dig, or the brute strength of cranes and loading equipment with which to carry stones that weighed up to 100 tons. And, how did they make their mathematical and astronomical computations so that the structures were built and placed with precision to exactly capture certain wondrous light patterns created by nature, such as the equinoxes? And why would the Great Pyramid of Giza be built to act like a beacon of light that can be seen even as far away into space as the moon?

Graham Hancock, a British writer and journalist who writes about ancient civilizations, developed a theory about a "mother culture" from which he believes all ancient historical civilizations began. His proposes that the conventionally accepted dates of all these ancient structures are actually older than what archeologists claim, for carbon 14 dating can only be used on things that were once living. There is room for error, which should raise doubts in your mind, or at least make you open to considering the possibilities. Clearly, there are things outside of what you learned in history class!

Hancock's theory can be scientifically grounded by the fact that most ancient structures were built on astronomical alignments that were present at the time, and that is an accurate way to date something. This is called Astroarcheology. For example, Giza pyramids exactly aligned with the rising and setting of Orion's belt at the time that alignment existed, which is a date that can be computed mathematically.

Knowledge of these alignments, together with our understanding of how these past alignments have since moved due to the 'precession of the equinoxes' relative to our present view of the heavens, presents a valuable tool to help us date these ancient structures. It should also make us question why these astrological alignments were so important to ancient cultures that they expended the time and effort to build structures that brought them into communion with the stars.

There is one explanation as to how ancient cultures with no visible evidence of having sophisticated building equipment could execute complex engineering principles using mathematical formulas like pi that had not yet been discovered to erect buildings that rival anything found on earth today.

Was Hancock's mother culture actually comprised of ancient astronauts? If so, what happened to them? Or are they still with us?

Perhaps one day we will know who these people truly were that ancient writings purport to have 'came from the stars'.

Made in the USA
Middletown, DE
17 December 2017